A SPARKLING TALE

JUDITH D GUNDERSON-CHRISTENSEN-DAVIS,
MICHAEL L GUNDERSON,
SHELLY J GUNDERSON-JENSEN.

authorHOUSE®

AuthorHouse™
1663 Liberty Drive
Bloomington, IN 47403
www.authorhouse.com
Phone: 1 (800) 839-8640

Published by AuthorHouse   03/28/2017

ISBN: 978-1-5246-8546-1 (sc)
ISBN: 978-1-5246-8545-4 (hc)
ISBN: 978-1-5246-8544-7 (e)

Library of Congress Control Number: 2017904735

Print information available on the last page.

Any people depicted in stock imagery provided by Thinkstock are models, and such images are being used for illustrative purposes only. Certain stock imagery © Thinkstock.

This book is printed on acid-free paper.

TO FATHER

FROM

YOUR CHILDREN

DEDICATED

To Mother

FOREWORD

If it's raining outside, or snowing, or thundering, or a hundred degrees, it would not deter father from a drive to any given location....in his car, van, motorcycle or motor bike.

If traffic was lined up for a mile, he would still go get in it.

If an area was flooded or a volcano had just erupted, he would drive through it.

All he would say is: "I just love it when it's like this"!!

That's the father of Judi, Mike and Shelly.

Best Father in the World.

He always lived A SPARKLING DAY!

No matter what.

This is the house father grew up in. It still stands today and those two palm trees on each side of the walkway to the door, are big and tall. The house looks much the same today too.

Phillip as a baby and youngster

Granny holding father...getting ready to go to church and getting the kids to stand still for a picture. Marguarite looking pretty. Father is front and middle.

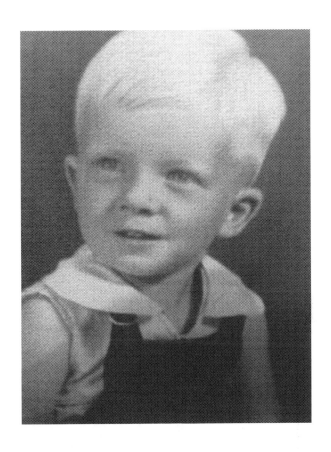

Granny calling......

Phillllllip!!!! What is in my washing machine? It's moving and it's not on!

OOOPS...I forgot about the snake so thinks Phillip. Guess that wasn't such a good place to put it.

Philllllip!!!!! Get these things out of the bathtub!

OOOPS, the tarantulas....darn, what am I going to do with them? I'll put them under my brother Tom's bed...just for now.

My granny, father's mother, had three boys, Harry, Tommy and Phillip and a daughter Marguerite. She had her hands full.

She worked at a packing house (Corona Sunkist) a tool place, (Corona Clipper) and then became a kindergarten teacher in Corona, at Jefferson Elementary School. They lived in a little three bedroom house on the skinniest street in Corona. (9ᵗʰ). Still to this day the house stands, much the same as in the 30's and the street is still the skinniest!! All the kids were born in Wisconsin except for father. He was born in Corona. Their daddy, Einar came from Oslo, Norway. He wasn't around much, but would visit every now and then to make sure the kids, especially Phillip, were behaving. If they needed a whooping, they got it.

Corona was small. It had a circle street called Grand Blvd and most of the city was inside of it in the early days. The outside of it was citrus. Father was energetic, adventurous and usually had a pack of dogs following him around. Barefoot with adventure in his head, he would take off after school, or sometimes during and go fishing in the Santa Ana River which was about three miles away. He walked just about everywhere on his bare feet. I imagine him as Tom Sawyer....but he was Phil....a one and only.

From a very young age he had his eye on a Corona girl named Shirley Lay. She stuck her tongue out at

him most of the time, but he was undaunted. She could roller skate better than him too.

During the winter he would go help to light the smudge pots in the citrus groves...most everyone who lived here would have to wear and hanky over their face so they didn't breath in the smoke. The front of that hanky would turn black.

Everybody walked to school just about and everybody knew everybody too. It was a quaint little town at that time.

Father worked. From a young age. When the soldiers came to town he would get them burgers and newspapers and deliver them to where they were stationed in town. One time he got them and they shipped out. He had a lot of burgers to eat and newspapers to read. More about this to come......

He had a bicycle at one point. He rode it everywhere. He visited Shirley a lot, but she told him to go away and leave her alone. Her phone number was 984J. He would never forget it! Then she would watch him leave until he was out of sight and think what a cutie he was. She told me that. He didn't know it at the time.

He raised pigeons for a while. His neighbor raised them too. He 'borrowed' some from his neighbor one time and put them in his cage and his neighbor told him his flew off. Ha. Father said he would sell him

some of his. Ha, the neighbor never caught on, but bought his back.

Father ran track. In 1944 he won at Jefferson Elementary School track meet,,,he was called the "blonde comet". He led the way and captured the annual track and field meet held for the four grammar schools in the Corona school district for the first time in the four year history of the meet. He piled up 18 points in winning the 100 yard dash, high jump and broad jump plus a second place in the hop, step and jump. After doing all that, he came back to anchor the winning Jefferson relay team to add more laurels to his already outstanding performance.

He thrived in his little Corona. Never a dull moment. He always had money in his pocket and he always had fun.

As Corona grew, so did he. The town got bigger, the freeway came along and grew to a monster. Old town Corona got ate up by new buildings and the groves disappeared as well and turned into housing tracks and golf courses. All the Gunderson towheads grew too and stayed in the town.

Harry, Harris Gunderson, had the TV shop. Gunderson's Sick TV's,,,

Tom Gunderson, once mayor of Corona, was a realtor.

Phil, always the Landscaper....and man of many talents you might say.

TRUE LOVE

Father courted Shirley and she still told him she didn't like him and to go away. But, he didn't and she married him.

Father was in the Forestry when he asked mother to marry him. She was going to dental assistant school in the San Francisco area and staying with her Uncle Fred and Aunt Evelyn. They lent them the money to get married and a suit for father. It broke her mother (Alma's) heart. Her only daughter got married in Clovis on August 14, 1950, without her. She so wanted to give her the 'dream' wedding.

FORESTRY

He was in the Forestry with his friend JC. They would drive from Corona and be at the barracks for weeks at a time. Father drove the fire truck and was in charge of crews. That's why he didn't get drafted because he was fighting fires. He learned a lot doing this and was fortunate not to get hurt. He did it for a few years then came back to Corona and started his life with Shirley.

Fathers 1948 Stick Shift Harley with suicide clutch.

He would put mother on the back of this thing and go to the mountains, beach and wherever he wanted, before the huge monster 91 freeway came about!! I don't know who the kitty is, and he doesn't remember either, but that kitty used to follow him everywhere! If he had his tool box open and was using tools, the kitty would sit in it and watch him. The kitty slept on the seat of the bike and waited for him to come out and get petted.

1936

One of Phil's first jobs, 5 years old, he raked leaves in yards....He would take his wagon with him to fill it up and after he did that, he would take his wagon to the groves and get some oranges. The wind would knock them off the trees a lot and most of them were good but wouldn't sale if they were picked up from the ground...

1938

He was a paper boy. His route was called route 31. He had a bicycle for this. He had a pet goat at this time in his life. He would hook his wagon up to the goat and then the goat would pull his doggy BoBo...this was so much fun...he had 7 other dogs...and at least five times a week he would hike to the river, about three miles from his house, to swim, fish and just play.

1939

Started raising chickens...had about 300 in 1940 he started raising them to sell to people to eat. He would get them ready to go for them. He also raised hens for eggs. He raised rabbits for a while as well. Then he got busy with the Army Camps in Corona. They moved in by the thousands. They were there where Village Grove is now. Also the East end of town and also where Cresta Verde is now. He sold them newspapers.

LA times, Corona Independent, and magazines. The papers and magazines were so heavy he had to use his wagon for this too. The Navy Hospital Bus was back and forth and the Hot Spot was the downtown Mava. He worked there as a janitor. The bus would carry about 25 people from Norco to Corona and to Anza. There was a very large Army camp in Arlington called Anza then...about 50,000 people. Then the bus would go to Riverside and then back to Corona. Home Gardens had only two houses and a little Road trolly that went back and forth from Riverside to Corona.

You would have to have stamps to get shoes and also stamps to get gas. You would get two stamps per year for shoes. And 3 and 5 gallon gas stamps. This was early 1940's.

Between 1935 to 1938....just to have fun, going to the River (Santa Ana) was the best. He would go to the Mexican Theatre. It was called Circle City Movies and on Saturdays it was English only. Best ones were Hop A Long Cassidy, Flash Gordon, ...Joe E Brown, Gene Autry, Roy Rogers, Dick Tracy.

Going to the Corona Plunge swimming was another fun thing to do. It was in the city park. Great entertainment on hot summer days.

Father had lots of friends. Enough for a football team. They could play that any time.

There was a bee yard in Corona in those years. Largest one in Southern California. Father would let the bees just cover him from head to toe...for fun!!! Judi

was allergic to bees! And that little tidbit just freaks her out!

Also in 1938 there was a big flood in Corona. It stopped all the traffic...flooded out a ranch at Prado Town...father used to go there to play with the a family there and eat the best Mexican food in town! They built the dam later and it broke at Fairmont Park in Riverside...

1943 is when he would smudge groves and fill smudge pots on cold nights for extra money. He also learned to graft citrus trees for extra money. He would get 3 cents a tree. He could do 200 a day. He started doing that 9 hours a day while he 14 and 15.

1945 he went to work at Gates Cactus Nursery in Norco, California (HorseTown USA). It was the largest cactus nursery in the United States at the time. He stayed there about a year.

Then he met a man who put him to work in palm tree sales. He went to Palm Springs, California, dug these trees up and trucked them back to Corona. $250 a tree.

1946 he worked at a winery capping wine bottles.

1947 he left there and went to Pacific Air Motive in Chino, California and worked on C-54 and C-47's. Then jets came in and you had to have 3 years of schooling...

That's when he went into the Forestry instead.

He also worked at some of the Southern California dairies doing all sorts of different things.

1950...he got married.

I think he loved little Shirley Grace Lay from the very first moment he laid eyes on her as children. I think the same of mother. I also think they were soul mates. He used to pick her up on his Doodle Bug (motor scooter) and they would go here and there and let their hair blow in the wind with great big smiles on their faces. Then he upgraded to a Cushman Scooter which was bigger and two speed....then that Harley got in there somewhere, then he got a Model A with a rumble seat, then a 1935 Ford which was real nice! As they went thru life together, he bought new vehicles every few years! But they always had a ride!! He had a comment about getting married at 19. "You don't know how young you are until you talk to a 19 year old at his present age (86). It's hard to believe it happened!"

1952 first baby was born, Judith

1953 he started landscaping. When it rained, he was a window washer.

1955 he started irrigation. That was the year child number two was born, Michael

Life was good for he and mother. She was frugal and smart with their money, so they always had a little something to play with, even if it was just a little extra gas money to take a Sunday drive. He worked hard and mother worked hard keeping a cozy home for him to come home to. They thrived. By 1960 they had their third child, Shelly.

XOXOXOXOXOXOXOXOXOXOX

We kid's had it good. We were happy, content, we were disciplined and well behaved.

We always went on Sunday drives it seems... Mountains, beach, desert, amusement parks...The weekends always held something fun to look forward to, as were all the holidays. Shelly and I twirled batons, we competed and have trophies and Judi even twirled for the LA Rams at one time. Mike and father raced

motorcycles. Father had a Honda SL 90 (#308) and Mike had a Yamaha 80. Mike has trophies too!!

Our parents kept us busy and happy and looking back, it's amazing just how much we had....and he worked all over Southern California. 1962 he even did a job at the famous La Brea Tar Pits. He did a job for the Institution of Oceanography in San Diego. He graded thousands of houses over the years, landscaped University of California, Riverside. He did pitch, he did a little town by Morro Bay and also even did a private golf course for Walt Disney. He has made baseball fields, basketball courts and even put up a huge metal building that became a batting cage building. Judi was his water girl while he graded the pad for that job! He has designed beautiful ponds, waterfalls and walking gardens and many rose gardens. He did the Ambassador Hotel in Los Angeles.

Then there was our own yard. We had a big front yard that was beautiful green grass, with a bench to sit on and look all the way to the mountains. Not now, 2017...there is a car dealer blocking everything!!!! But our backyard, was a kid's dream. We didn't have to play in the street, or stay inside to play video games, we didn't need cell phones...we had grass, paths in the yard to ride tricycles and bikes, we had a swing set with a sand box...brother had a tree house, we had a field behind the house where we could build forts when the grass got high, we had a patio we could spend hours on playing with our toys, eat....we had dog runs...we had dogs, cats, a goat at one time...a

duck, chickens, a rooster....pigeons, pea-cocks....we had tetherball, basketball, an area to play baseball and football...we had swimming pools for the summer... and mother always had her clothesline. We had mud to play in and eat, like brother did, and mother had a sundeck over the swing set so she could tan and sunburn. Father had a work shop. Mike stole that at one point and changed all of father's color coded tools to a different color. Hence they became Mike's tools. We had turtles and a BBQ pit at one time. We had bushes we could make forts in too. All in one back yard that was always well maintained. There were accent lights on bushes and ornamental palms...it was beautiful. We picked up our toys and put them away when we were done playing with them. We got good and dirty as much as we could.

It was wonderful! At Christmas, father would decorate the front and win the Corona house decoration trophy almost every year they judged that. We had mild delivered and the Helms truck would come and mama would buy bread, sometimes pies and almost always donuts. We had no side- walks, but that didn't matter one bit. We had a white picket fence around the front too! We also had an incinerator in the back to burn our garbage. Yep, it was indeed wonderful and life was good....Father was the best there is and mama was the best there was and us kids....we were the best then and we are the best now in my eyes....all three of us are stable, happy, contented and healthy and truly blessed.

Also, father loved deep sea fishing. It was his hobby. He would get home from work and drive to Davy's Locker and take the night boat out. He would catch Albacore and have it canned. Great tuna. Yellowtail and other fish. Would also fish in Mexico and got himself a great big Marlin.

At one point, his mother got somewhat famous. Here is the story about that.....

THE ARTICLE

In 1966, the Saturday, October 29th edition of the Corona, Norco newspaper, The Daily-Enterprise, did an article on Fathers mother titled, Movie stirs fond memories. This is the article word for word, written by staff writer Iris Hayward.

Old movies never die—they just go on television. And because they do, retired Corona teacher Myrtle Florence Gunderson is being reminded of a memorable period in her teaching career.

The period was her four tenure as a teacher at Rhinehardt School in Benson Corner Wisconsin.

Although the experience was 45 years ago, Mrs. Gunderson remembers it as if it was yesterday. Even if she didn't remember, Hollywood wouldn't let her forget.

The school, and Mrs. Gunderson as its teacher, received fame of a sort through a movie made over 20

years ago: "My Vines Have Tender Grapes" starring Margaret O'Brien and Edward G. Robinson.

The movie was recently shown over a local television channel and is liable to crop up again before it runs its course.

Mrs. Gunderson watched it once, which she said was enough. "I didn't feel as if it was really me," she said, "but I know it covered the time I was at the school, and it was my name."

A MATTER of fact she didn't know a part of her life was immortalized in a movie until it was pointed out to her by a member of her family.

Mrs. Gunderson's maiden name was Johnson and it was as "Miss Johnson" she was known in the movie.

Mrs. Gunderson said she believes the movie was taken from a book which was written by someone with one of her students of the period.

She was born in Amherst, Wisconsin which had a population of 600 and had not grown since.

Although Rhinehardt School was only a few miles from her home town, the young teacher (she was 17 her first year of teaching there) boarded near the school. There were no cars in those days and in winter everything was snowed in.

(this was not in the article..or the movie..if she was at home and had to get to school, she learned to ice skate, so she could cross a pond that was closer than walking miles to get over a bridge).

Miss Johnson enjoyed it though. "I was so young and I had so much fun there. You just turned the key and ran off to a dance at the end of the day."

Mrs. Gunderson came to California 35 years ago, and has lived in the Corona area ever since. She taught for 11 years at Jefferson School, 10 of them in kindergarten. Of her teaching day's she says simply, "I loved it." She still receives visits from some of her former Corona students, who are now grown.

The movie tells story of a little boy, a little girl, her father and school days in a rural community. Some of the ages and incidents were changed around, Mrs. Gunderson said, but there's no doubt about the identity of the people involved.

"The story is about a little girl, Selma Jorgensen, who went to the school," Mrs. Gunderson said. "I'm not positive Selma went to school with me, but there were other girls in the family and her sisters did.

"Their father was really awfully good to those girls. He grew apples and towards the end they showed the beautiful orchard."

"In the movie they had the little boy-Arnold Henson-aged five, and he wasn't in school. Actually, Arnold went to school when I taught there. He and Selma lived across the street from each other."

He was the cutest thing you ever saw. I'm sure they had the same boy in mind."

"It was just lovely teaching there. I always had a Christmas program and had to give it three nights because everyone wanted to see it."

"One year I had to dress Arnold like a little girl because I was short one girl. He was so cute and offered to do it."

There was also a retarded girl in the story, Ingebor, who was quite a bit older than I. She worked where I boarded."

Mrs. Gunderson did take exception to one thing about the Miss Johnson in the movie. "It said the teacher fell in love with an editor. I didn't know there even was an editor."

The movie was truthful about something else, though. "It tells how I disliked the country, and I did. I always have disliked it. When I went back to visit last summer, I thought, "I'm going to the country and I have to make the most of it." But all I thought when I got there was, 'My, the chickens have sure grown.'"

Mrs. Gunderson has four grown children of her own: Harris, Margarite, Tom and Phil. Harris and Tom own Gunderson's TV; Phil owns Gunderson Landscaping.

Mrs. Gunderson said she saw the old Rhinehardt School when she visited Wisconsin this past summer. Not only is the old one-room structure still standing, but the log cabin which preceded it is also standing, next to a marsh.

The old log school was finally moved and a more sturdy structure built in 1868. The first teacher was Peter P. Iverslie, who received $100 for five months' work. His room and board bill for this period was $40.

The names of the teachers down through the years all reflected the Scandinavia descent of the people living in the area.

By the time Mrs. Gunderson became teacher, (with over 50 students) the pay scale at Rhinehardt School had gone up to $50 a month.

"We had Polish children and children from all kinds of backgrounds," Mrs. Gunderson recalls. "It was hard. I would like to see any teacher today go in and teach like that. But I liked it."

End of article........

Our granny had a cousin Marion, in Norco who had an egg ranch on Hillside Ave. Father sometimes would work on the ranch for her.

LEFSE

Every year for the holidays, granny would make Lefse. This a a Norwegian sort of potato tortilla... it's good, and all of us Gunderson kids still make it. Granny would sometimes make it all by herself, which is quite a chore. Here is father, always the roller in 2014. In 2016, I made it all by myself. First time.

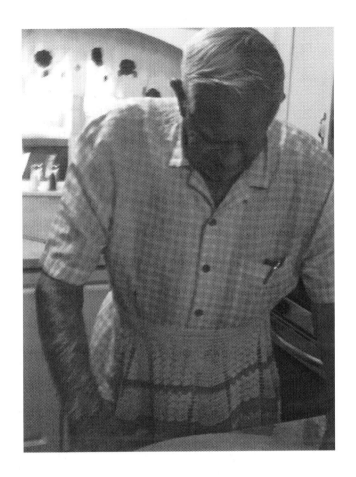

This was at brother's house. I would usually just come along to be the taster of the first warm pieces that were made....My niece Michelle has it down pat, the size of the dough balls to be rolled. It's good stuff!!! Though, not everyone thinks so.

And here's our pa and ma in 2010 after 60 years of marriage.

These two rooted, grew, endured and survived those years.

He lost his 'Squirley' December 26, 2010......a stroke.

XOXOXOXOXOXOXOXOXOXOXOX

MORE REVERIE

They used to bowl too. Corona used to have a nice Bowling Alley and it was right next door to my girlfriend Karen's house. Her parents bowled too, but they didn't bowl with mine. I think everyone in Corona may have bowled.

When pa and ma bowled, sometimes they would leave us kids in the kid room...there was a 'babysitter' in it and toys and it was noisier than the alley's they bowled on. I didn't like it. I was older and there wasn't anything to do. So, I told the babysitter lady that my mommy and daddy said it was okay if I went out and sat at a booth and watched the bowlers. She let me. When mama saw me she said "what are you doing out here" and I told her the babysitter said it was okay for me to come out there and sit. Well, that was two lies and when I got home that night, mama put some Zest soap on my toothbrush and brushed my teeth with it. It was awful and to this day I won't use Zest!!! When we were riding the rails together she denied doing this....I don't know why she can't remember it.

I sure can!!!!! Not to mention, I will never forget that taste!

Corona eventually tore that bowling alley down and there is a dental building there now. Ugly!!!

We used to go to Santa's Village in our mountains. Every year I think. They had a deer petting area. You could go right into the fenced area and feed the deer by hand. Of coarse Santa was there too. The bakery, well, you can just imagine what was in that....with hot cocoa, just yum!!! That eventually closed as well, tho, recently reopened....there was usually snow when we went. Snow was too cold for me and one of my family members threw a snowball in my face, then took a picture. I was 5 or 6 and I am crying in that picture.

I didn't like snow too much....and it hurt I guess...and to be living in it now, well, it's beautiful at first...then it gets to be a hassle!!!

Those were the days, as the saying goes.

They also had a house on the beach in Mexico in the '70s....in those years father had his office in a lighthouse.

Shelly got to spend a lot of time there and I would drive down in my little Porsche to visit when I was dating my future husband Chris. Mike would be down there almost every weekend. It was great place and mother always had a fresh tan. After all three of us kids were gone and out on our own, they bought a motor home and traveled quite a bit around the United States. Mother loved motor homing. She also loved Boston Terriers. She had five at different times and collected every knick knack she could find on them, including bedding, towels, clothes...they were everywhere, even in the motor home. First, she had Pino, then Peni, the Bumper, then Ginger, then Jeepers. Whenever we saw the folks, we saw a little black and white thing with them.

Mother and Judi also traveled Amtrak...Judi wrote a book about the travels called "Mama" and The Autumn Train.

JUDI on JUDI

Then I lost my husband Chris of 40 years in 2012 and ended up moving just a few doors down from father. From July 2012 to January 2016, the two of us became best friends and learned how to be a widower and a widow, somewhat gracefully. He would drive by my house every morning at 4:40 on his way to the coffee shop. When I wasn't working, I would make sure I was up....Ha!!! had to set my alarm for that. Every time he drove by when he wasn't working later in the day he would pick me up and we would go on adventures...rain, snow, sleet...haha, will not the latter two...we went on daily drives..he back seat was set up for his dogs....they had a little apartment in back and we would just go. Everywhere we went too he would see something that reminded him of jobs he's done and sometimes they were jobs he did. We went to the mountains, the beach, the desert...we would just take off and see where we would end up. I saw a whole lot of South Califorinia I hadn't seen before and a lot that I hadn't seen in a really long time. We would get Double Double's at In and Out, tacos at Del Taco and Taco Bell....sometimes we would even go to regular restaurants and eat...we were all into the fast food....also, he would cook...he would make concoctions in his crock pot that were usually really tasty and I would drive my little golf cart down to his place. We both had golf carts, as we were living in a nice little vintage mobile home park. He would either

come eat my concoctions or I would eat his...either way...we were together at some point almost every single day. Even when we watched TV, we would call each other and make comments on something we were watching...our favorite being Judge Judy. We had fun together...we would go shopping for him mostly and sometimes for me. He was quicker than I liked but it was fun and I could find things for him in the stores that he couldn't find. At Christmas I would put up mothers little faux tree the day after Thanksgiving. Father would come up and help me get the lights on. Then I would cover it solid with ornaments where you couldn't even see the tree. Early Christmas morning he would drive his golf cart down at 4 in the morning and we would open our presents...he would bring his little dog with him and we would drink coffee and make a big mess in the living room. It was so much fun. Then later in the day we would go be with the whole family and whoever's house it was at.

Then something happened that was totally unexpected. My girlfriend from 2nd grade on passed away. I used to go visit her in Oregon...I had been there 4 times to visit her and her husband Bill. I thought, now I've lost three people I love and was not very happy about it. This was in 2014. Around Christmas that year, Bill called me and we talked and talked about our spouses we had lost. Long story short...we fell in love over the phone. Most unexpected indeed. He came down from Oregon and married me on January 30, 2016 and packed me, my dog Andy

and my cat Molly up and all of us in my Lincoln, and whisked me away to Oregon.

As much as father and I were going to miss each other, father bravely walked me down the aisle at my friends Steve and Jeanne's house and gave me away to Bill. He was so happy that his daughter was entering a new chapter in her life.

He drove up in his motor home in September as did Mike and his wife Chris, and visited. I wanted to keep him!!! I am so lucky, Curt and Shelly came up first...Even my ex-boss Leroy and His wife Sylvia have been to visit, Steve and Jeanne have been here and, my niece Michelle and her girlfriend Krista too!! Its only a 14-15 drive. It is now 2017 and I just experienced my first winter in Snow. As it happens, we got so much snow it almost covered our whole house. I have never seen so much snow in my whole entire life. Andy seems to do just fine in it and I am thankful I don't work and have to drive in it.

I had a bit of a rough start when I got up here...I rolled a 700 pound quad over on top of me. I had to be air lifted off the mountain I was on to the hospital. I was in the hospital for a week with 5 broken ribs, a broken sternum and a punctured lung. I am still healing from this, but so very lucky to be alive and getting back to normal. Not a day goes by that I don't thank God for my life and the many blessings I have bestowed on me. I also thank Him for my father who is such a light in my life.

Every single morning at 3:30am I get up. At 4, I call father and we talk anywhere from 10 minutes to over an hour. There is always something new to talk about with him. I couldn't start my day if I didn't have him to talk to.

And Bill, he is the most wonderful man on earth as far as I'm concerned. He treats me like a Princess and puts a smile on my face every day. I am so lucky. And father likes his son in law too!!

I love Oregon. I love getting up in the morning and I love going to bed. I love my house. I love looking out the windows. Everywhere I look out them there is deer. Sometimes there is a herd of 30 or more. Bucks, does, fawns. I will never ever tire of this. They're beautiful. Poor things have had a rough winter with all their plants that they eat being covered in snow. I can watch them from my recliner. I've watched the bucks poke each other with their antlers and chase the girlies. It is so en'deering'....

We have gray squirrels too. When the snow was up to the bottom of the windows, the squirrels come right up and look inside. They are so cute. I love watching them too...they just run around with the deer. Birds... we have lots of them too. Raccoons, pine squirrels and everyone has dogs and we live in the woods where they have horses too. When Andy saw his first horse, I could barely hang on to him. I don't know what he

thinks about the deer but he chases them out of our yard and they just gracefully glide over the fence.

I have learned to stack wood. We had 6 cords to stack this year. I haven't cut kindling yet, though father is all for me having my very own ax. Also, I have learned to walk with chains on my boots so I don't fall on my butt on ice.

As well as talking to father on the phone every day, I also write him several letters a week and load pictures off my phone onto the computer and send him pictures of everything too. Even the chains on my boots!! He writes to me too. I never in my wildest dreams thought I would be writing to my father every week! I love that too!!

A CONTENTED FATHER STILL HAVING FUN!!!

He always has a sparkle in his eyes that make you know the minute you see him that all is well and he is going to make you laugh and learn at the same time when you're with him. His infectious laugh and teasing manner is also forthright and genuine. Ya have to listen to him sometimes too because when he is explaining something, he is telling you how to do something that you need to know about. There were times growing up us kids would hear him talk, but not really listen. We thought we knew more than our parents did because we were sure they just didn't understand. Ha, boy were we ever dumb!! Now we hang on every word even though, we three all agree that indeed, some of father's tales are not only sparkling, but also 'tall' as well!!

Visiting Judi in Oregon

AND,,,,,,his Gpee.....

Here he is sitting in my kitchen in Oregon when he came to visit. I still called him at 4 and then went out and got him and brought him in.

MORE PICTURES OF THE MAN WITH
THE TWINKLE IN HIS EYES

He has had over 40 cars in his lifetime......by the way!!!!!!

Working on his car in front of the Old Corona High School.

SOMETIME IN THE 1960'S....GROWING.....

HAVING FUN....................

His Family

Father, Granny, Harris, Margaurite and Tommy

FOUR GENERATIONS

OF>>>>>>>>>>>>>>>>>>>>>>>>>>>>>>

GUNDERSON BOYS

FATHER, GPEE, MICHEAL, ADAM AND MIKE

1961

A HAPPY GUY

2000

A HAPPY GUY STILL!!!!!

2014

HELPING JUDI GET HER LIGHTS ON THE TREE
OH WAIT......ON HE..................

JUST LIKE GRANDPA

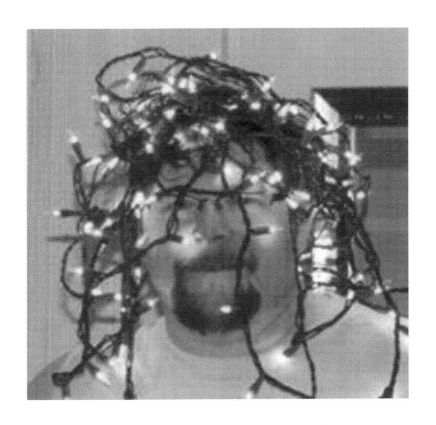

MUST BE A GUNDERSON THING..............................!!

2015

HE AND GPEE

2015

JUDI AND FATHER

2017...

Father, aka, Mr. Phillip Gunderson, grandpa, uncle, daddy, papa, Dad and DoDa.....he is all that and we all think he is just absolutely the greatest.

His grandchildren, Michael, Michelle, Christopher and Katrina.

His great-grandchildren, Patrick, Sidney, Elliana, Adam, Abigail, Brooklyn and Chase.

This is not The End.

He still doesn't know what he going to do when he gets old. Right now, he just has as much fun as he can with a big smile and twinkle in his eye.

Every day is a "Sparkling Day"…..

Yep….that's my DoDa

And…..just for fun….a few currently taken pictures taken in March of 2017….my first visit in over a year to visit him and family in California…..

Showing a picture of his family. The only two we can identify is uncle Selmer bottom first, left and Granny,

bottom second to last. Those ladies could be her sisters, which I am thinking they are. Not sure of the guys.

Just goes to show one, that if you don't write on every picture you have so that future generations don't have to wonder. Although the wonder of it all is somewhat alluring and we starve for knowing where we come from. Maybe somebody will figure out who everybody is someday by the future computers. We have come a long way and expect to go further....Right?? Yep!!

Trying out the seat on the back of his trike. Thinking of going for a ride in May...I fit just fine!!!

The trike was bigger than I thought. So all I can say about that is, Vroom Vroom!!!!!

Tho, I don't really care much for the helmet!!!!!

Visiting father this March was a fun and exciting time. We went for drives everyday the first week. Ate a lot of fast food, my favorite being the Double Double at In n' Out.….Sundaes at McDonalds, tho was hoping for banana splits at Dairy Queen. Our fav DQ was gone though!!

Never a dull moment with my DoDa…..

As I end my story of father, it is not really the end. He is a constant source of adventure and stories. I talk to him just about every day….actually it IS every day….at 4 in the morning. I set my alarm for 3:30 am so I am sure to call on time. This is his "best time to call time"….we both start a day with a positive outlook…. and sometimes if something happens during the day that we want to share, we call each other…just for a moment or so…we both like to watch Judge Judy and sometimes we have to call while watching just to laugh out loud.

My father is just the best there is.....86 and still young!

Printed in the United States
By Bookmasters